Piranhas

by Conrad J. Storad

Lerner Publications Company • Minneapolis

To my nephews Austin and Ryan and nieces Katelyn and Taylor. Never stop learning!

The images in this book are used with the permission of:
© Norbert Wu/ www.norbertwu.com, p. 4; © Nature's Images, Inc., pp. 6, 9, 10, 12, 13, 26, 30, 32, 35, 39, 47, 48 (bottom); blickwinkel/Schmidbauer/Alamy, p. 7; © jochem wijnands/Picture Contact/Alamy, p. 8; Visual & Written SL/Alamy, p. 11; © Jany Sauvanet/Auscape/DRK PHOTO, p. 14; © Paul A. Zahl/National Geographic/Getty Images, p. 15; © Claus Meyer/Minden Pictures, p. 16; © Nik Wheeler/Danita Deimont Agency /drr.net, p. 17; © Thomas L. Kelly/drr.net, p. 18; © Claus Meyer/Tyba/drr.net, p. 19; © Andre Seale/age fotostock/Photolibrary, p. 20; © Tony Crocetta/NHPA/Photoshot, p. 21; © Konrad Wothe/Minden Pictures, p. 22; © Morales Morales/age fotostock/Photolibrary, pp. 23, 27; © Biosphoto/Hubert Yan/Peter Arnold, Inc., pp. 24, 46; © Tom Stack/Tom Stack and Associates/drr.net, pp. 25, 43; © Amazon-Images/Alamy, p. 28; © David Shale/naturepl.com, p. 29; © Chris Catton/Photolibrary, p. 31; © Jan Aldenhoven/Photolibrary, p. 33; © SeaPics.com, p. 34; © Berndt Fisher/Oxford Scientific/ Photolibrary, p. 36; © WILDLIFE/ Peter Arnold, Inc., p. 37; © Redmond Durrrell/Alamy, p. 38; © Joel Sartore/National Geographic/ Getty Images, p. 40; © Bruce Farnsworth/ PlaceStockPhoto.com/drr.net, p. 41; © Nilton Ricardo/ BrazilPhotos/drr.net, p. 42.

Front cover; © Paul A. Zahl /National Geographic/Getty Images.

Lerner Publications Company
A division of Lerner Publishing Group, Inc.
241 First Avenue North
Minneapolis, MN 55401 U.S.A.

Website address: www.lernerbooks.com

Library of Congress Cataloging-in-Publication Data

Storad, Conrad J.
    Piranhas / by Conrad J. Storad.
        p.   cm. — (Early bird nature books)
    Includes index.
    ISBN 978–0–8225–9433–8 (lib. bdg. : alk. paper)
    1. Piranhas—Juvenile literature. I. Title.
QL638.C5S86 2009
597'.48—dc22   2008026605

Manufactured in the United States of America
1 2 3 4 5 6 – BP – 14 13 12 11 10 09

Contents

Piranhas live in South America in rivers and lakes of the Amazon River basin. The yellow areas show exactly where piranhas live.

SOUTH AMERICA

Be a Word Detective

Can you find these words as you read about the piranha's life? Be a detective and try to figure out what they mean. You can turn to the glossary on pages 46–47 for help.

carnivores ✓

drought ✓

feeding frenzy ✓

fry ✓

herbivores ✓

omnivores ✓

prey ✓

scales ✓

scavenge ✓

school ✓

scutes ✓

5

Chapter 1

These are piranhas. Where do piranhas live?

The Piranha

A small fish with big eyes swims through the shallow river. It is hunting for something to eat. The fish has sharp teeth. Spiky skin runs along the fish's orange belly. But what is this toothy fish? It's a piranha (peh-RAHN-uh)!

Piranha is not the name for one kind of fish. It is the name for a family of fish. Piranhas live in South America. There are more than 20 different kinds of piranhas.

Many kinds of piranhas live in South America. This kind is called piraya. *It is one of the largest kinds of piranhas.*

This piranha was caught in a river in South America.

Piranhas are not large fish. The average piranha is just 8 to 12 inches (20 to 30 centimeters) long. That is about as long as a sheet of notebook paper. The largest piranhas can grow to more than 24 inches (61 cm) long. That is as long as a full page of the newspaper.

Different kinds of piranhas have different body shapes. Many piranhas have rounded heads. Their bodies are flat but thick. Other piranhas have oval-shaped bodies.

This piranha is called an elongated piranha. It is long and narrow. Many other kinds of piranhas have an oval shape with short, rounded faces.

Piranhas come in many colors. There are white piranhas and black piranhas. Some are silver. Some have olive green or bluish black bodies. Others have red or orange bellies. Still others have spots or stripes along their sides and on their fins.

Most red-bellied piranhas have red bellies. But red-bellied piranhas in southern Brazil are yellow, like this piranha.

Piranhas are covered with small pieces of hardened skin.

Piranhas have small scales on their bodies. Scales are small pieces of hardened skin that protect the fish's body. Piranhas have two types of scales.

The scales on this piranha look as if they sparkle.
This kind of piranha is called a Sanchez's piranha.
Sometimes they are called diamond piranhas.

One type is round with smooth edges. It has no color. These scales shed easily from the outside layer of a piranha's skin.

The second type looks like a row of saw teeth along the piranha's belly. These scales are called scutes. They also help protect the piranha.

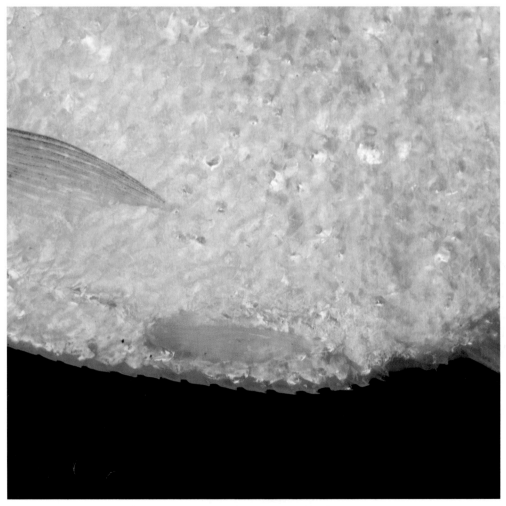

The piranha's belly has a row of scales called scutes.

Piranhas have lots of razor-sharp teeth. Each tooth is shaped like a triangle. Thick, fleshy lips cover the teeth. A piranha's lower jaw sticks out below the upper jaw. The teeth fit together like puzzle pieces. They form a sawlike edge. The jaw muscles are very strong. They can open wide and snap shut quickly to chomp on food.

The word piranha *comes from native South American languages. "Piru" means "fish." "Rahna" refers to teeth. Together, the words mean "toothed fish," or "fish with teeth."*

Most piranhas live in muddy water.

The piranha's eyes are set on each side of its flat head. The fish can't see well straight ahead. But great vision is not important for them. Piranhas often live in murky, muddy water. It is hard to see in these dark waters. A good sense of smell is much more important.

Piranhas have an excellent sense of smell. Piranhas also can sense tiny movements. Other fish sometimes splash and make noise in the water. Piranhas can feel the movement in the water.

Piranhas have four nostrils that help them smell. They use their sense of smell to find food. Scientists think piranhas can even smell blood.

Chapter 2

These boaters travel on the Amazon River in South America. In what kind of waters do piranhas live?

Home and Food

Piranhas are freshwater fish. They can't survive in salty ocean water. Rivers and lakes make excellent homes for piranhas.

The Amazon River basin covers more than 2.7 million square miles (7 square kilometers). That is almost as big as the mainland United States.

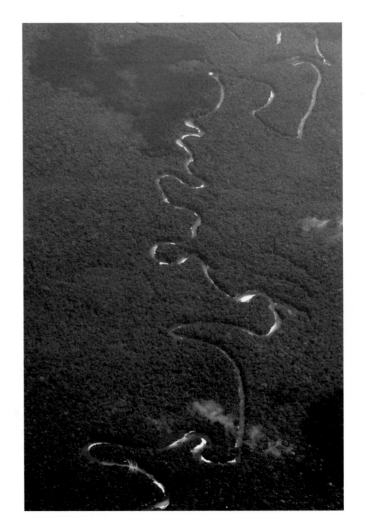

Piranhas live in rivers and lakes in the Amazon River basin. The Amazon River basin is a large area of land. It includes the Amazon River and many other smaller rivers, streams, and lakes.

A piranha swims after a baby river turtle. Some piranhas eat animals or other fish.

Piranhas find plenty of food in the Amazon River basin's waters. Some piranhas eat other fish. They might also eat shrimp, insects, and small snakes. These piranhas are carnivores (KAHR-nuh-vohrz). Carnivores are animals that eat meat.

Other piranhas eat fruits and berries that fall into the water. They eat bits of plants that grow in the water too. These piranhas are herbivores (HUR-buh-vohrz). Herbivores are animals that eat plants.

Some piranhas eat plants or seeds. Piranhas use their sharp teeth to bite off pieces of the plants they eat.

A piranha waits in the murky river water. River plants and fish can be food for the piranha.

Most piranhas eat almost anything that comes their way. They eat fish, berries, fruits, and other foods. These piranhas are omnivores (AHM-nih-vohrz). Omnivores are animals that eat both meat and plants.

Both meat- and plant-eating piranhas are good at finding food. Meat-eating piranhas are quick, savage hunters. Sometimes a meat-eating piranha will hide near plants or rocks. It waits for prey to swim close by. Prey are animals that are hunted and eaten by other animals.

The weeds and plants at the river bottom make good hiding places for fish.

Piranhas use their senses to find sick or dead animals that fall into the water. These animals make good food for piranhas.

Wham! The attack is over in less than one second. It happens so fast that it is hard to see. The piranha has chomped into the flesh of its prey.

Piranhas will eat food that they find in the water.

Piranhas don't always chase down prey when they are hungry. Piranhas also might scavenge (SKAV-uhnj) to find food. This means they look for food that other animals have left behind. Both meat- and plant-eating piranhas scavenge.

Meat-eating piranhas scavenge for dead animals. They will eat dead fish and the bodies of dead animals.

Plant-eating piranhas may scavenge for leaves or seeds left behind by other animals. They look for these foods on the bottom of a lake or river.

Catfish are another fish that scavenges to find food.

Piranhas are not picky eaters. They'll eat almost anything that they can find. No food goes to waste around a hungry piranha!

Piranhas even eat other piranhas. This piranha's fins were eaten by another piranha. But this usually does not kill the fish, and the fins will grow back.

Chapter 3

A group of red-bellied piranhas swim together. Why do piranhas stay in groups?

Piranha Schools

Piranhas swim around in groups. A group of piranhas is called a school. Scientists aren't sure why piranhas swim in schools. Schools may keep piranhas safe. Hunting animals may find it harder to attack a group of fish.

These piranhas swim side by side in a school.

A piranha will swim close to other members of its school. But not too close. If another fish gets too close, the piranha will wag its body from side to side. Or it will chase the other fish. Piranhas do not like other fish to swim behind them.

A school might include 20 piranhas. Or it could include many more fish. Different types of piranhas have different-sized schools.

A school's size also depends on how much water is in the river or lake. When there is less water in the river or lake, piranhas don't have much room to swim. The fish bunch together in larger schools.

A large school of piranhas travels together. When fish do not have room to spread out, they swim closely together.

There is less water during a drought (DROWT). During these times, there is little or no rainfall. The water level in rivers and lakes gets low.

Men stand in a shallow lake in the Amazon River basin. During the dry season, the water drops, and fish are crowded together.

When a school of piranhas attacks its food, it is called a feeding frenzy.

Piranhas are most dangerous during droughts. The fish bunch together. It becomes hard to find enough food. Starving piranhas will attack and eat almost anything just to stay alive.

Chapter 4

This is a young black piranha. Black piranhas do not get their dark color until they get older. What else happens to baby piranhas as they grow?

From Egg to Adult

Piranhas build nests when they are ready to have babies. Mother and father piranhas work together. They scoop out a shallow hole in the sandy bottom of a lake or river. Sometimes they line the hole with leaves or bits of plants.

The mother piranha lays 700 to 4,000 tiny eggs in the nest. The eggs look like a sticky mass of jelly. Each tiny egg is only an eighth of an inch (0.3 cm) long. That is smaller than a sesame seed. Some of the eggs stick to the leaves or plants in the nest.

Piranhas grow darker in color when they become adults. When they are grown, they lay eggs that hatch.

This is a nest made by bluegill sunfish. Bluegills, like piranhas, sweep out a nest with their tail fins.

Both mother and father piranhas try to protect the eggs. But some eggs break loose from the nest material. These eggs float away. They are quickly gobbled up by other fish. Eggs that stay in the nest are hidden and safe.

In two to nine days, baby piranhas hatch from the tiny eggs. Baby piranhas are called fry. The fry are less than half an inch (1 cm) long. They have sharp teeth. They are ready to eat the moment they hatch. Fry feast on shrimp, worms, and insects.

Baby piranhas eat a lot. The 1-inch-long (2.5 cm) black piranha (left) just ate part of another fish's tail.

Lots of fry get eaten by other fish. Adult piranhas sometimes eat the fry. Birds, snakes, and baby crocodiles also eat them. The fry even eat one another! Many fry live for only one day or less.

Many fry become food for other animals. This crested caracara holds a piranha in its beak.

This fry will be full grown in only two years.

The fry that live grow quickly. They become full-grown piranhas in about two years. Then they can have fry of their own.

Chapter 5

Many people are afraid of piranhas. Are piranhas really dangerous to people?

People and Piranhas

Many people think piranhas are dangerous. It's true that piranhas do bite other animals and sometimes people.

Piranhas can and do attack people. Some of the stories are true. But people are not a natural prey for piranhas.

Many people who live in the Amazon basin are not afraid of piranhas. Piranhas usually do not hurt humans unless the fish are hungry or in danger.

People who fish for piranhas are at most risk of being bitten. The most dangerous piranhas are the ones flopping around in the bottom of a boat. They can bite off the fingers or toes of careless fishers.

A piranha can bite through a thin steel fishing hook. People fishing for piranhas need to be very careful with the piranhas they catch.

A man in Ecuador eats a piranha. Piranhas are a popular food in South America.

Piranhas don't often harm people. But people often hunt piranhas. Some people in South America catch and eat piranhas. They are a very popular food.

Piranhas are fascinating creatures. This interesting fish should not be the reason for nightmares. One thing is certain. Many more piranhas are eaten by people than the other way around.

Many markets in South America sell piranhas as food.
These piranhas were caught from the Amazon River.
This man is decorating them for sale.

Piranhas are difficult to study. Scientists are still learning new things about piranhas. What will they learn next?

A NOTE TO ADULTS
ON SHARING A BOOK

When you share a book with a child, you show that reading is important. To get the most out of the experience, read in a comfortable, quiet place. Turn off the television and limit other distractions, such as telephone calls.

Be prepared to start slowly. Take turns reading parts of this book. Stop occasionally and discuss what you're reading. Talk about the photographs. If the child begins to lose interest, stop reading. When you pick up the book again, revisit the parts you have already read.

BE A VOCABULARY DETECTIVE

The word list on page 5 contains words that are important in understanding the topic of this book. Be word detectives and search for the words as you read the book together. Talk about what the words mean and how they are used in the sentence. Do any of these words have more than one meaning? You will find the words defined in a glossary on page 46.

WHAT ABOUT QUESTIONS?

Use questions to make sure the child understands the information in this book. Here are some suggestions:

> What did this paragraph tell us? What does this picture show? What do you think we'll learn about next? What colors are piranhas? Do they have lots of teeth? Where do piranhas live? Do you want to have a piranha as a pet? Why, or why not? What is your favorite part of this book? Why?

If the child has questions, don't hesitate to respond with questions of your own, such as What do *you* think? Why? What is it that you don't know? If the child can't remember certain facts, turn to the index.

INTRODUCING THE INDEX

The index helps readers find information without searching through the whole book. Turn to the index on page 48. Choose an entry such as *scales*, and ask the child to use the index to find out what scales do for piranhas. Repeat this exercise with as many entries as you like. Ask the child to point out the differences between an index and a glossary. (The index helps readers find information, while the glossary tells readers what words mean.)

LEARN MORE ABOUT
PIRANHAS

BOOKS

Berendes, Mary. *Piranhas*. Chanhassen, MN: Child's World, 1999. Learn more about piranhas and their habits in this book.

Dollar, Sam. *Piranhas*. Austin, TX: Steadwell Books, 2001. Read about piranhas and where they live.

Schulte, Mary. *Piranhas and Other Fish*. New York: Children's Press, 2005. This book has information about piranhas and other kinds of fish that live in lakes, rivers, and oceans.

WEBSITES

Kids Corner: Animal Guide-Red Piranha
http://www.georgiaaquarium.org/animalguide/riverscout/redpiranha.aspx
This website will help you learn all about red piranhas, one of the many types of piranhas in the world.

Red-Bellied Piranhas
http://www.sheddaquarium.org/red_bellied_piranhas.html
The Shedd Aquarium in Chicago is home to red-bellied piranhas. This site tells about the fish that live in this aquarium.

GLOSSARY

carnivores (KAHR-nuh-vohrz): animals that eat meat

drought (DROWT): a period of time when there is little or no rainfall

feeding frenzy: excited attack on food by a group of piranhas

fry: a baby piranha

herbivores (HUR-buh-vohrz): animals that eat plants

omnivores (AHM-nih-vohrz): animals that eat both meat and plants

prey: animals that are hunted and eaten by other animals

scales: small pieces of skin that cover and protect a fish's body

scavenge (SKAV-uhnj): to look for food that other animals have left behind. Both meat- and plant-eating piranhas scavenge.

school: a group of piranhas

scutes: another type of scale on a piranha's body. Scutes look like saw teeth on a piranha's belly.

INDEX

Pages listed in **bold** type refer to photographs.

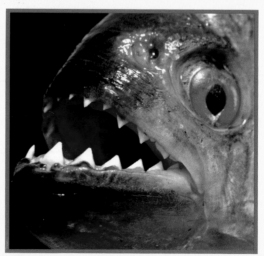